Numbers 0-20 Activity Book

for ages 4-5

This CGP book is bursting with bright and colourful Maths activities for children in Reception.

It's a brilliant way to introduce the numbers 0-20 — and it's stacks of fun too!

Helpful Hints

- A grown-up can help you read the questions. Let them know what you've been learning at school.

- Find a nice place to work. Make sure you're comfortable at your desk or table.

- Use a pencil to write or draw your answers. You can use coloured pencils to colour in the pictures.

- Work neatly, and try to keep your pencil inside the lines.

- Writing the numbers nice and clearly is really important — you can practise this on a separate piece of paper.

- The 'Roman Jumble' activity in the centre covers the numbers 0 to 20 — you may want to save this until last.

Published by CGP

ISBN: 978 1 78908 835 9

Editors: Emma Clayton, Sean McParland, Rachael Rogers, Tamara Sinivassen

With thanks to Sharon Gulliver and Duncan Lindsay for the proofreading.
With thanks to Lottie Edwards for the copyright research.

Printed by Elanders Ltd, Newcastle upon Tyne.
Cover and graphics used throughout the book © www.edu-clips.com
Cover design concept by emc design ltd.

Text, design, layout and original illustrations
© Coordination Group Publications Ltd. (CGP) 2021
All rights reserved.

Photocopying this book is not permitted, even if you have a CLA licence.
Extra copies are available from CGP with next day delivery • 0800 1712 712 • www.cgpbooks.co.uk

Contents

The Numbers 0 to 3	2
The Numbers 4 to 7	4
The Numbers 8 to 10	6
The Numbers 0 to 10	8
The Numbers 11 and 12	10
The Numbers 13 and 14	12
Roman Jumble	14
The Numbers 15 and 16	16
The Numbers 17 and 18	18
The Numbers 19 and 20	20
The Numbers 11 to 20	22
Number Lines	24
Ordering Numbers	26
Odd and Even Numbers	28
Tropical Trail	30

The Numbers 0 to 3

How It Works

How many balloons are on each stand?

There are **0** balloons on this stand.

There is **1** balloon on this stand.

There are **2** balloons on this stand.

There are **3** balloons on this stand.

Now Try These

Join the dots to write the numbers.

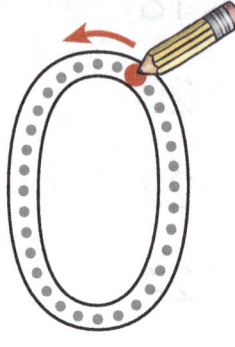 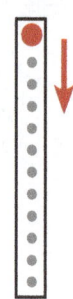 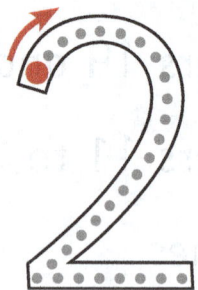 

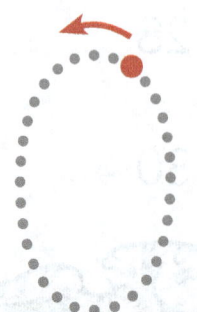   

Which hat has **3** spots? Tick the box.

 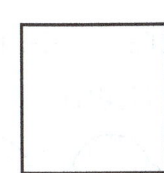  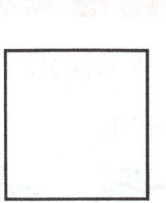 

Draw a line to match each juggler to the number of balls he has.

1 ball   2 balls   3 balls

How many of these things can you see in the picture below?

   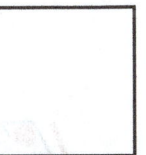 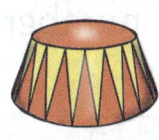  

You're off to a great start! Put a tick in the box.

The Numbers 4 to 7

How It Works

Here are **4** apples.
Count them.

Here are **5** ice-creams.
Count them.

Here are **6** flowers.
Count them.

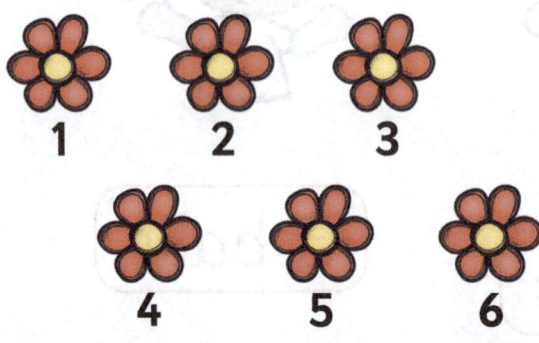

Here are **7** stars.
Count them.

Now Try These

Join the dots to write the numbers.

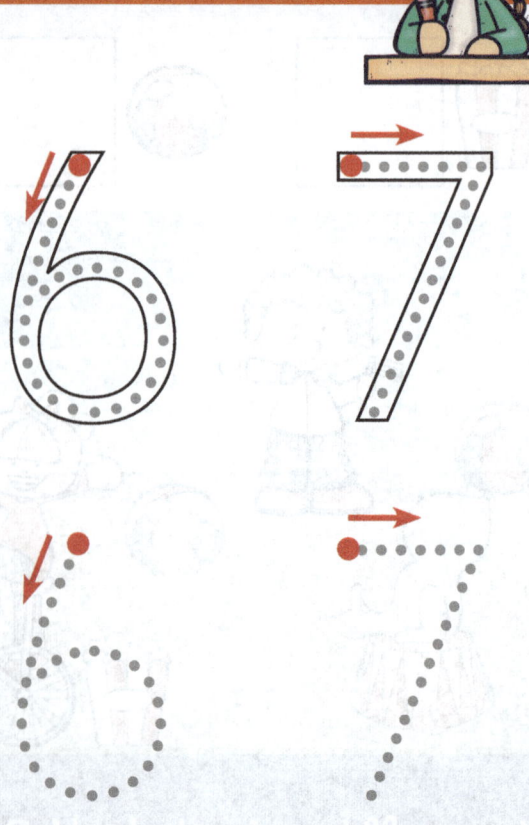

Colour in penguin number seven.

Count the hearts on each card.
Draw a line to match each card to the correct number.

4   5   6

How many balloons does each child have?

 balloons

 balloons

Yay! You know the numbers 4, 5, 6 and 7! Tick the box.

The Numbers 8 to 10

How It Works

Here are **8** footballs. Count them.
1 2 3 4 5 6 7 8

Here are **9** whistles. Count them.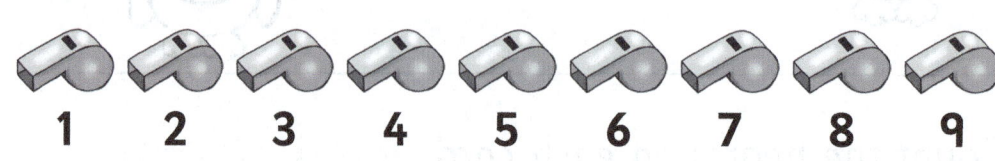
1 2 3 4 5 6 7 8 9

Here are **10** trophies. Count them.
1 2 3 4 5 6 7 8 9 10

Now Try These

Join the dots to write the numbers.

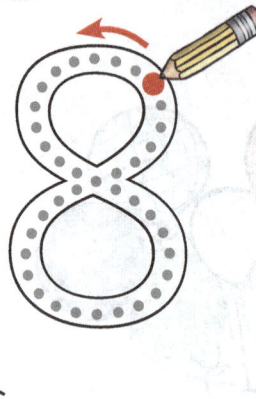 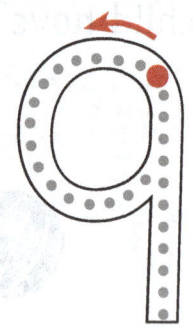 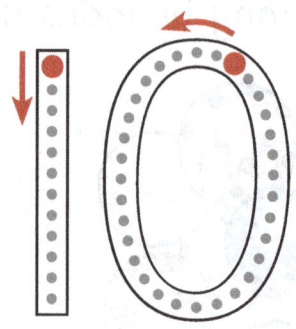

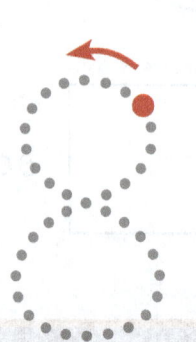 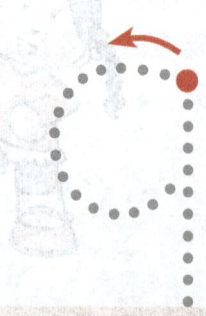 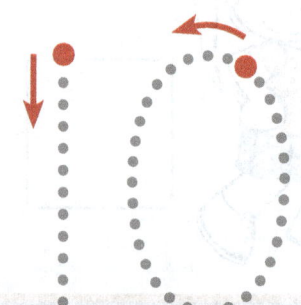

Colour in the referee's cards that have an eight on them.

Draw lines to match each ticket to the right seat.

 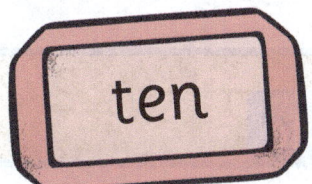

 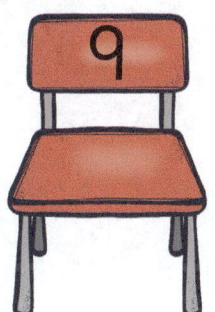

Look at this football team. How many players are there?

players

You're doing really well! Tick the box.

The Numbers 0 to 10

How It Works

Here are the numbers 0 to 10. Say each number out loud.

Now Try These

Join the dots to write the numbers.

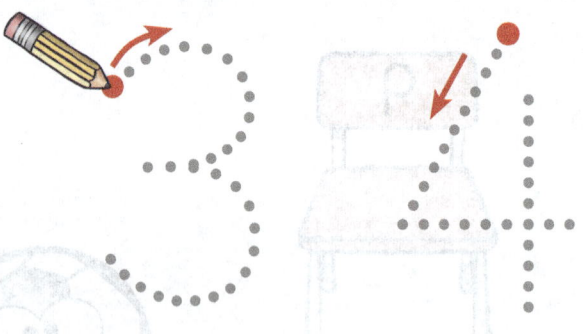 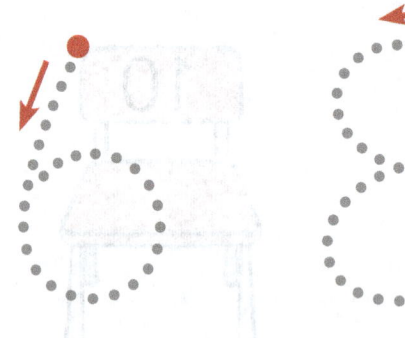

Tick the partners that both have the same number.

Draw lines to match the dice to the correct numbers.

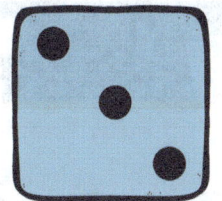 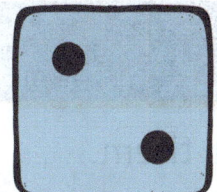 

   [2]   [3]   [5]

Colour all the plates that have a number one in one colour.
Colour all the plates that have a number nine in a different colour.

How many flowers are in each basket?

☐ flowers   ☐ flowers   ☐ flowers

Well done! You've earned a tick in the box!

The Numbers 11 and 12

How It Works

Here are **11** mittens. Count them.

Here are **12** hats. Count them.

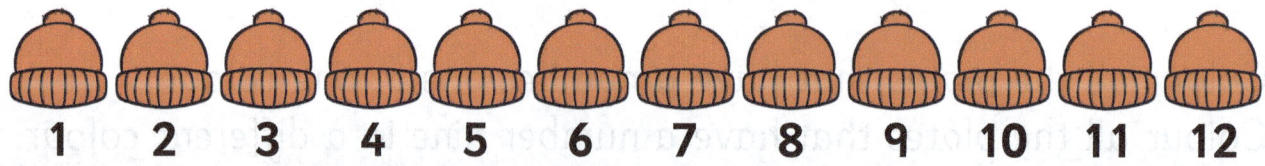

Now Try These

Join the dots to write the numbers. Then have a go without dots.

How many feathers are there? Tick the correct box.

11 ☐

12 ☐

Colour in 11 mugs.

Draw lines to match the skaters to the numbers.

How many muddy paw prints are there?

How many paw prints are there altogether?

If you're fantastic with 11 and 12, give the box a tick!

The Numbers 13 and 14

How It Works

Here are **13** spoons. Count them.

Here are **14** frogs. Count them.

Now Try These

Join the dots to write the numbers. Then have a go without dots.

Circle all the cards that show a number thirteen.

13   3   14   12
14   10   13   14

Trace the paths to find who painted the number fourteen.
Put a tick next to their name.

Jack

Maisie

How many bubbles are there? Circle the number.

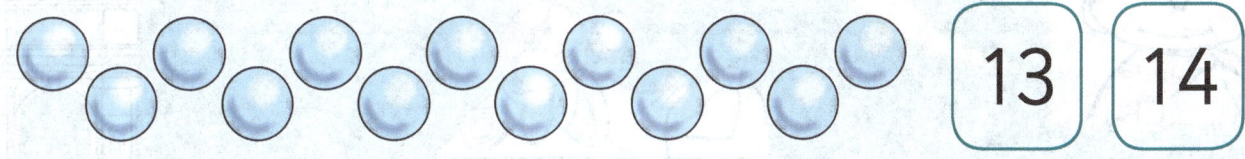

13   14

How many flowers are in each field?

flowers

flowers

Colour the rabbit in the field that has **more** flowers.

That's numbers 13 and 14 sorted! Tick the box.

Roman Jumble

Oh no! Felix and Julia dropped their coins and got them all mixed up.

Use their clues to help you match them to their coins on the next page.

 One of my coins has the number thirteen on it.

One of my coins has the number that is one less than eight on it.

 The missing number from this number line is on one of my coins.

5   6   7   ●   9   10   11

The coin with the number seventeen on it is mine.

 The number of grapes on this bunch is on one of my coins.

 The number covered by the helmet is on one of my coins.

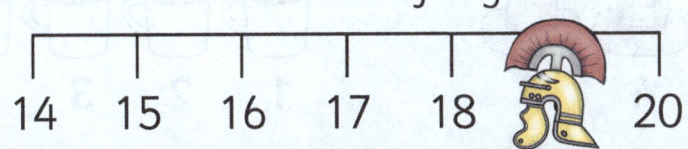

Draw lines to match each coin to the right person.

The Numbers 15 and 16

How It Works

Here are **15** hats.
Count them.

Here are **16** mugs.
Count them.

Now Try These

Join the dots to write the numbers.   Then have a go without dots.

Tick the box next to house number sixteen.

Trace the path that starts with fifteen.
Circle the dog at the end of that path.

How many snowflakes are there altogether?

snowflakes

Brilliantly done! Give that box a tick.

The Numbers 17 and 18

How It Works

Here are **17** buttons.
Count them.

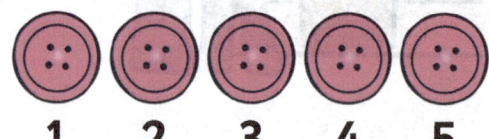
1 2 3 4 5

6 7 8 9 10 11

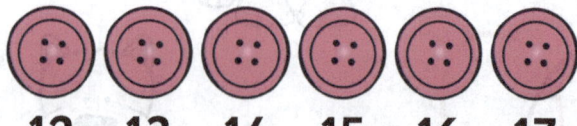
12 13 14 15 16 17

Here are **18** monsters.
Count them.

1 2 3 4 5 6

7 8 9 10 11 12

13 14 15 16 17 18

Now Try These

Join the dots to write the numbers. Then have a go without dots.

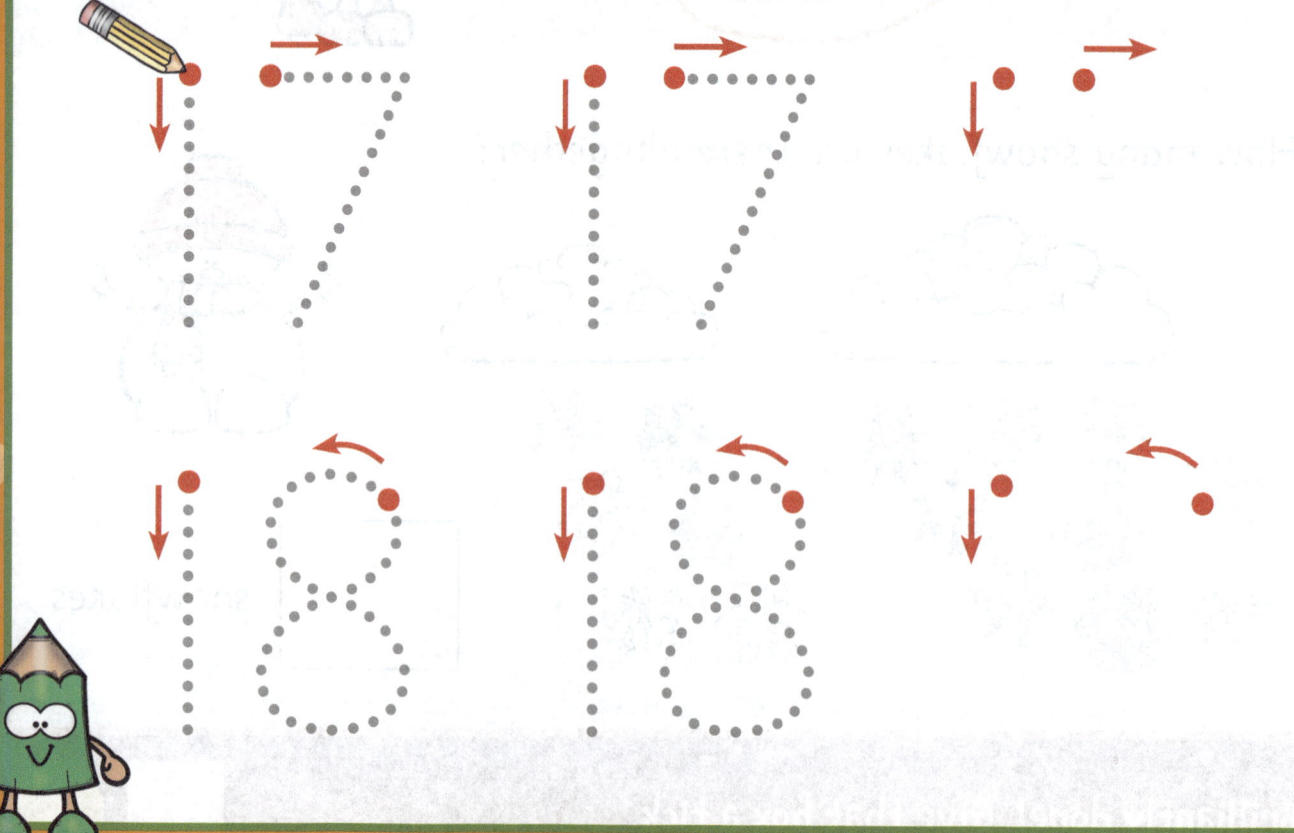

Circle the book where the two numbers match.

Colour in all of the instruments with eighteen on them.

How many paintbrushes are there in this picture?

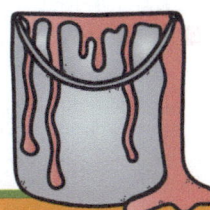  paintbrushes

You're great with 17 and 18! Tick the box.

The Numbers 19 and 20

How It Works

Here are **19** pigs.
Count them.

1 2 3 4 5

6 7 8 9 10

11 12 13 14 15

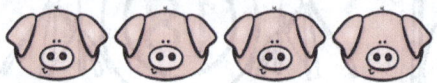
16 17 18 19

Here are **20** bananas.
Count them.

1 2 3 4 5

6 7 8 9 10

11 12 13 14 15

16 17 18 19 20

Now Try These

Join the dots to write the numbers. Then have a go without dots.

How many eggs are there altogether?

Circle the number that is **one more** than the number in the mouth.

Colour in all of the bugs with twenty on them.

Wow, superb work with 19 and 20! Tick the box.

The Numbers 11 to 20

How It Works

Here are the numbers 11 to 20. Say each number out loud.

| 11 eleven | 12 twelve | 13 thirteen | 14 fourteen | 15 fifteen |
| 16 sixteen | 17 seventeen | 18 eighteen | 19 nineteen | 20 twenty |

Now Try These

Join the dots to write the numbers.

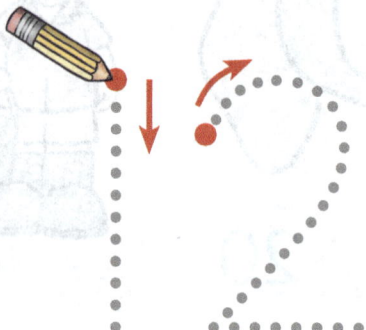   12   14   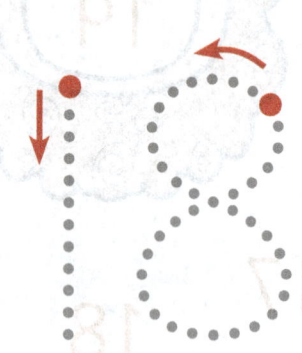 18

How many fish are there in each group?

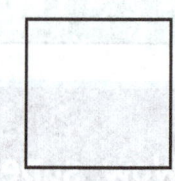

Circle 13 starfish.

Count the gems. Tick the box if the number on the treasure chest matches the number of gems.

Draw lines to match each number to the correct boat.

Super job! Pop a tick in the box.

Number Lines

How It Works

A **number line** shows you a line of numbers in the right order.

Which number is missing from this number line?

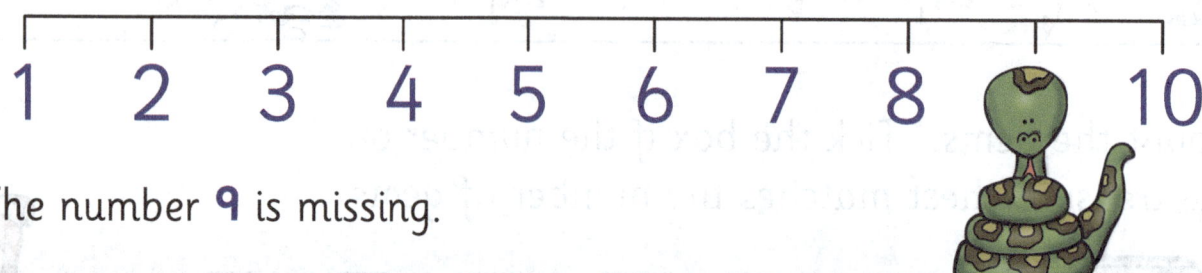

The number 9 is missing.

Now Try These

Circle the person holding the number that is missing from this number line.

Colour in the number that is in the wrong place on this number line.

24

Fill in the missing numbers.

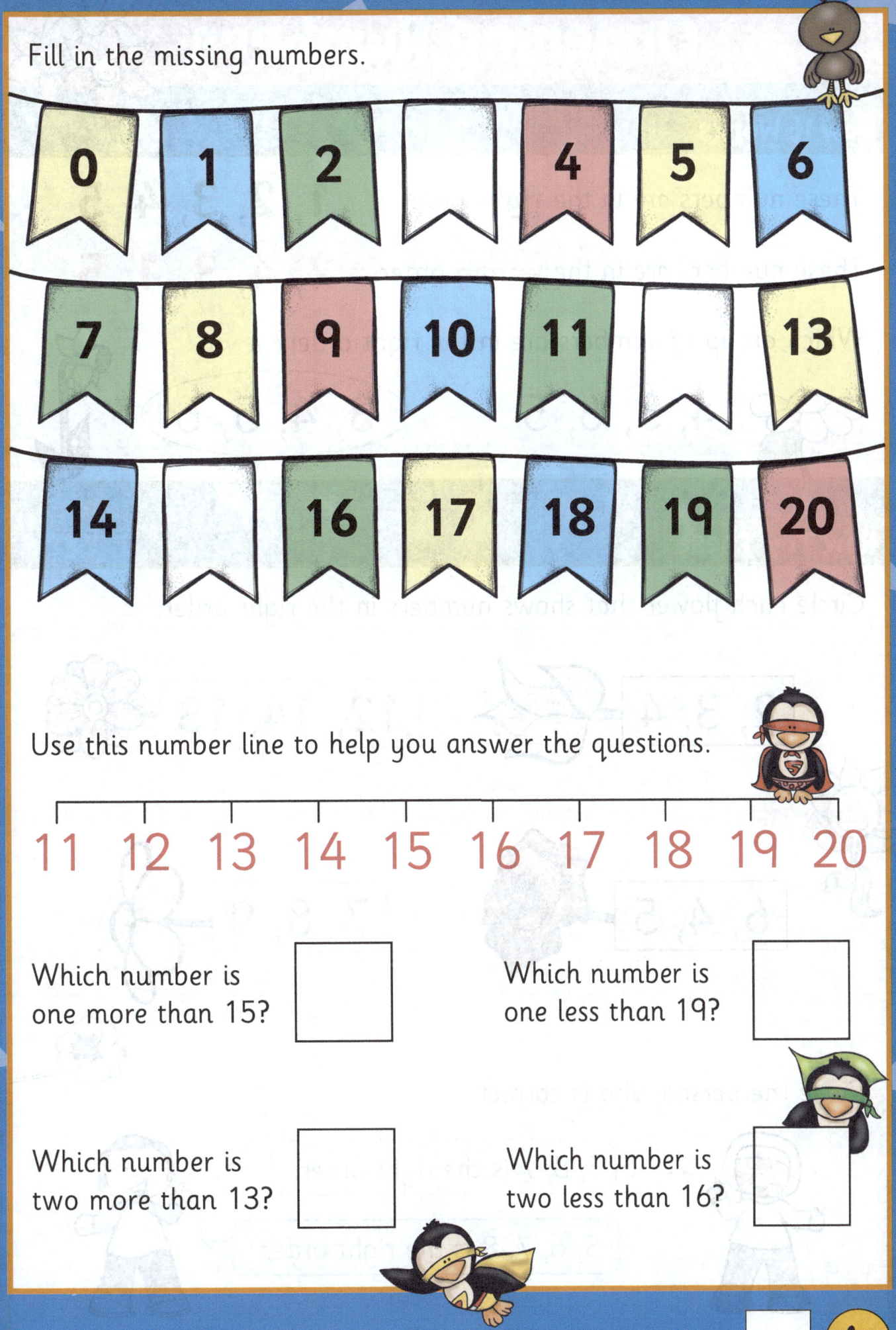

Use this number line to help you answer the questions.

11 12 13 14 15 16 17 18 19 20

Which number is one more than 15? ☐

Which number is one less than 19? ☐

Which number is two more than 13? ☐

Which number is two less than 16? ☐

You're a number line hero! Tick the box.

Ordering Numbers

How It Works

These numbers are in the **right** order: **1, 2, 3, 4, 5**

These numbers are in the **wrong** order: **2, 4, 3, 1, 5**

Which group of numbers are in the right order?

 4, 3, 6, 5   (3, 4, 5, 6)

Now Try These

Circle each flower that shows numbers in the right order.

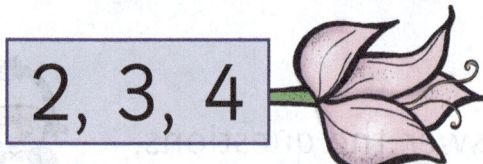 2, 3, 4    12, 14, 13

 6, 4, 5    7, 8, 9

Circle the person who is correct.

 6, 5, 8, 7 is the right order.

5, 6, 7, 8 is the right order.

What do these balls look like in the right order? Tick the box.

The numbers on the train are in the right order.
Colour in the driver with the missing number on his hat.

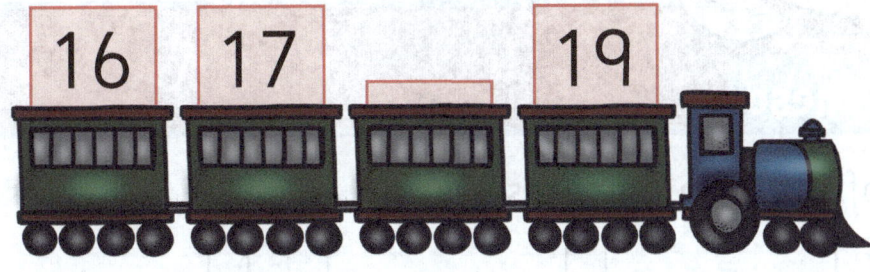

Write the numbers in order.

If you're an expert at ordering, then tick the box!

Odd and Even Numbers

How It Works

Some numbers are **odd** and other numbers are **even**.

These numbers are **odd**: 1 3 5 7 9

These numbers are **even**: 2 4 6 8 10

Now Try These

Tick all of the even numbers.

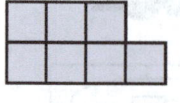  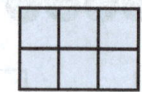 

Colour in all of the trees with odd numbers on their trunks.

Circle all of the keys with odd numbers.

Draw lines to put each drop of water into the correct bucket.

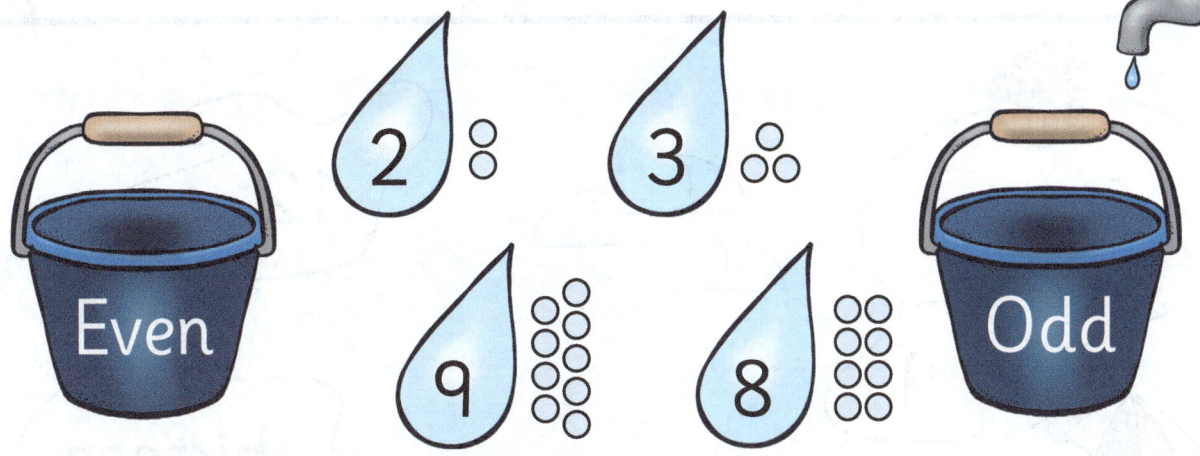

Copy the even numbers from the planets onto the flag.

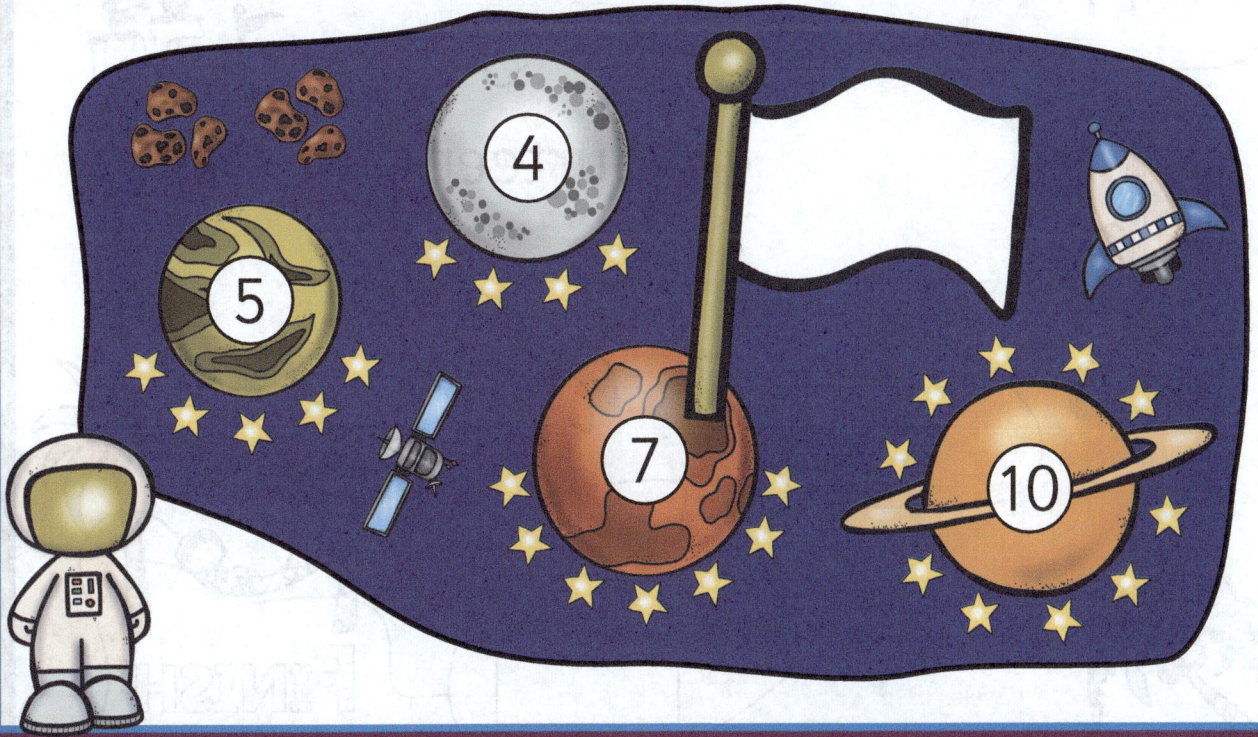

Fantastic job — even I'm impressed! Tick the box.

Tropical Trail

Draw a line to connect the islands in the right order.
Fill in the missing number as you go.

Use this number line to help if you need it.

9 10 11 12 13 14 15 16

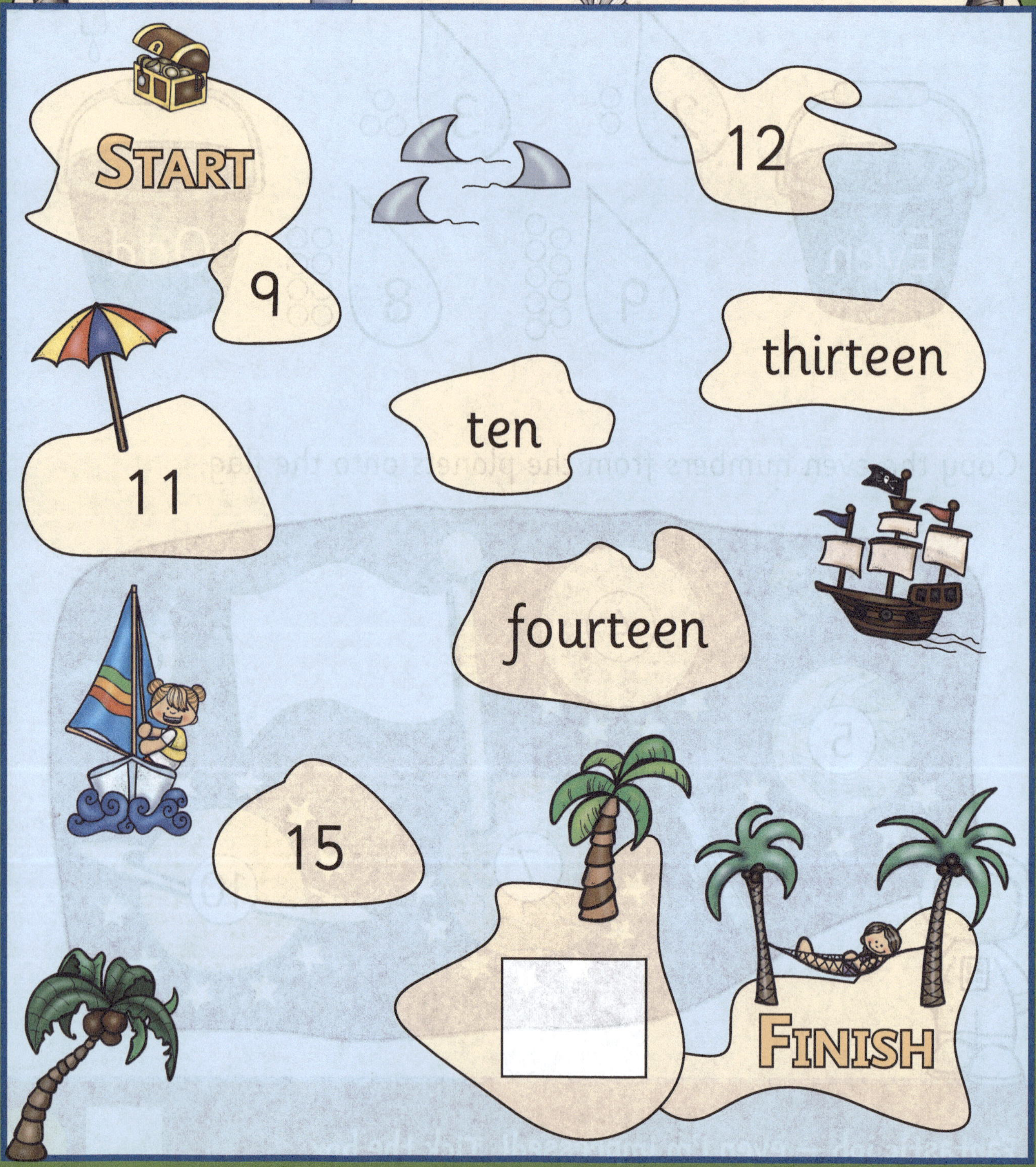

START
9
11
12
thirteen
ten
fourteen
15
FINISH